Hidden Treasures

Hidden Treasures

A Weekly Devotional and Prayer Journal for Women

Sharon Pankey

© 2012 by Sharon Pankey. All rights reserved.
2nd Printing 2014

Trusted Books is an imprint of Deep River Books. The views expressed or implied in this work are those of the author. To learn more about Deep River Books, go online to www.DeepRiverBooks.com.

No part of this publication may be reproduced, stored in a retrieval system, or transmitted in any way by any means—electronic, mechanical, photocopy, recording, or otherwise—without the prior permission of the copyright holder, except as provided by USA copyright law.

The author of this book has waived a portion of the publisher's recommended professional editing services. As such, any related errors found in this finished product are not the responsibility of the publisher.

Unless otherwise noted, all Scriptures are taken from THE HOLY BIBLE, NEW INTERNATIONAL VERSION®, NIV® Copyright © 1973, 1978, 1984, 2011 by Biblica, Inc.™ Used by permission. All rights reserved worldwide. www.zondervan.com

Definitions are from: © 2011 Merriam-Webster®, Incorporated.

ISBN 13: 978-1-63269-087-6
Library of Congress Catalog Card Number: 2011932295

For every woman whose hands lay ahold of this book, may you pursue the One who sees you as the apple of His eye.

Contents

Acknowledgments xi

Devotionals
   The Purple Tulip 1
   A Simple Faith 4
   Simply Trust. 7
   A Perfect Wisdom 10
   Perseverance, My Child 13
   Till the Land 16
   Called to Pray. 19
   The Gift. 22
   Not Guilty 25
   God of the Living. 28
   David's Supplication 31
   Close the Door. 34
   Pay Attention 37
   Selah 40

Still the Same	43
A Hope that Unfolds	46
The Wait Is Over	49
The Promise	52
Suddenly	55
A Place of Rest	58
Hall of Faith	61
The Unexpected	64
He Knows	67
Finding Truth, Walking in Freedom	70
The Rolling Away	73
Ordinary Man, Extraordinary Prayer	76
A Cry in the Night	79
A Declaration of His Faithfulness	82
An Inexpressible Joy	85
Living in Obedience and Blessed	88
Wandering in Disobedience and Cursed	91
Rejoice!	94
Life	97
Are You Willing to Wait?	100
A Light Shining in Darkness	103
The Discipline of Fasting	106
Secret Place	109
Rules of the Game	112
Pass It On	115
The Voice	118
Resurrection Power	121
For His Glory	124
His Holiness	127
Hannah	130

His Faithfulness Endures Forever 133
Snooze Button 136
The Fountain 139
Nothing New 142
Family Tree 145
Standing in the Gap 148
A Steadfast Heart 151
Display of Glory 154
The Promise Fulfilled 157

Acknowledgments

SHANNON, SASHA, SHAYLA, and Shane, I love you so much, you are my treasures from God.

My editor, B. Kay Coulter, whom I truly believe God sent my way. Thank you for partnering with me.

> "I will give you hidden treasures,
> riches stored in secret places,
> so that you may know that I am the LORD,
> the God of Israel,
> who summons you by name."
> —Isaiah 45:3

My Sister,

In this garden of love between the Creator of the universe and His precious daughters stands the most vital relationship that you will ever have on this side of eternity.

As with any garden, water and exposure to the sun is necessary for growth. Likewise, God's Holy Word and a vibrant prayer life are essential in the life of His beloved daughters.

I pray that this prayer journal will cause you to experience an abundance of growth in your walk with the One who knew you before the foundations of the earth. I pray that where there is darkness, He will shine His light upon you. I pray that His living water will saturate your heart now and forevermore.

His forever,
Sharon Pankey

Devotionals

The Purple Tulip

"In the morning, LORD, you hear my voice;
in the morning I lay my requests before
you and wait expectantly."
—Psalm 5:3

IN MY ATTEMPT to develop a green thumb, I started a flower garden. What a joy it has been to watch my "pretty in pink" geraniums bloom. One night, as I was sitting on my porch, something caught my eye. I couldn't believe it, but there it was, standing tall and majestic in a sea of all pink, a purple tulip! As I stood there totally perplexed as to where this flower came from, God spoke ever so gently to my heart: "It's been growing all along." As I pondered that for a while, I began to realize that in my own life there have been many petitions that I have placed before our Creator, sometimes even becoming faint from praying and waiting for His perfect timing. But, just when I think that nothing will come to fruition, He speaks…

and when He does I can't deny it. He reminded me through the purple tulip that while I have been in prayer, He has been at the root of my prayer all along, watering it, causing it to grow and finally, allowing it to spring forth. The amazing part of it all is that it seemed to happen suddenly, but to God, it was all in His perfect timing.

Beloved, how are you praying? Are you anticipating that the God of all creation will answer? Are you aware that while you are praying, He is actively moving on your behalf? Worship Him while you wait, and be prepared for how He chooses to answer...you will be amazed!

The Purple Tulip

A Simple Faith

"Elijah was a human being, even as we are.
He prayed earnestly that it would not rain,
and it did not rain on the land for three and a half years."
—James 5:17

IF YOU ARE anything like me, you marvel at all of the great stories of faith found in God's Word—the stories that leave you standing in awe of God's promises and the faith of those chosen to walk in them. So I asked myself, if I claim to have faith, then why I am not seeing a move of God like those in His Word? If God is the same yesterday, today, and forever, then what is the true condition of my heart? The writer of Hebrews reminded me that without faith it is absolutely impossible to please Him, and if anyone comes to Him they must believe that He is real and He rewards those who earnestly seek Him. I am reminded of the prophet Elijah, who earnestly prayed that it would not rain and it did not rain—a simple prayer with a simple faith. Elijah was a man with the same DNA makeup as you and I. He possessed the same emotions that we do. He had desires, fears, sadness, and happiness. But, something was different. He possessed a simple faith in an extraordinary God. When he prayed, he believed the God of the universe heard him and would answer.

Beloved, can the same be said of you and me? Are you praying with a simple faith? When you pray, believe and watch Him move! As you pray, remove the doubt that He is not there and embrace the truth that He is very near to you and hears your every word.

Hidden Treasures

Simply Trust

> "Trust in the LORD with all your heart and lean
> not on your own understanding."
> —Proverbs 3:5

"LORD, IT'S TRULY in Your hands"…these are the very words I have uttered so many times after I have laid everything before the Father in prayer. This is the place where the burden has been lifted, where I have laid it all before the throne of grace and mercy. I arise and move forward in confidence that the God of heaven and earth has heard my every petition and wiped away every tear. Oh, such a sweet place of surrender. It is a place where God expects me to rest in Him, trust in His timing and in His way, to remove my limited understanding and apply His Word over my life, to worship Him while I await His answer. This is the step that I so often stumble over, yet it is the most comfortable place in our walk with God. Psalm 23 reminds us that God is the One who makes us lie in green pastures and leads us beside still waters. This is where He wants us, a place of complete surrender…a simple trust. Something so simple, yet we make it so complicated. Mark 10:15 says, "Truly I tell you, anyone who will not receive the kingdom of God like a little child will never enter it." There's something to be said about the simple trust of a child, the innocence and the hope, the expectation of receiving His very best simply because the child asks.

Spend some time praying for God to remove any hardness of heart and revive your hope in Him. Because He knows your weaknesses, simply ask Him to help you trust again…He will!

Simply Trust

A Perfect Wisdom

"But the wisdom that comes from heaven is first of all pure;
then peace-loving, considerate, submissive,
full of mercy and good fruit, impartial and sincere."
—James 3:17

WE LIVE IN a high-tech society, with laptops and cellular phones that can do just about anything. Even the GPS systems are now able to give live traffic updates no matter where you are. If you have access to the Internet, you can use any popular search engine and find information on any subject in a matter of seconds! Technology is ever-changing and you have to keep up with it or else you will get lost. Don't get me wrong, I love the benefit of living in the digital age, so no complaints here. But, as God's children, we have access to Someone who never changes, who is our Source for information. We have access to a wisdom that trumps any search engine. This wisdom is never wrong and offers a life of peace, mercy, and blessings. His wisdom brings health to our bodies. His wisdom is unchanging. Because He is an intimate God and desires relationship more than anything, He wants us to come to Him for every matter under the sun. The Word of God is living and active. Whatever you need in this life, He has the answer.

The Word reminds us not to conform to the age in which we live but to be transformed by the renewing of our minds with the daily application of His Word. (See Rom. 12:2.)

As you pray, take inventory of your heart. Are you putting His Word first? Are you making His Word your source? Remember, the result of yielding to His wisdom is priceless.

Hidden Treasures

Perseverance, My Child

"Let perseverance finish its work so that you may be mature and complete, not lacking anything."
—James 1:4

I REMEMBER A time when, pregnant with my first child, how I savored every moment of that precious child taking up residence within me. Every movement, every doctor's appointment, and even those dreaded symptoms that came along with the miracle of pregnancy. Even at the very end, at a time when most women were ready for an exit strategy, I didn't want it to end. However, I also remember being pregnant with my second and third children. I must admit my perspective changed a little. Now the symptoms were unbearable, the movements hurt, and instead of wanting it to last forever, every day was a prayer to please hurry this along! It was often in those times when a veteran mom would gently remind me of the precious fruit in my womb that needed time to grow. What a remarkable similarity with our prayer life. In the beginning stages of our relationship with God, our prayers are often vibrant and full of hope. Time goes by and we have weathered some storms, we have had our hearts broken, we have been pruned, and we have hit the valleys and the mountains. We get to a place where the wait seems unbearable. We wonder if our prayers are making a dent in heaven's gates. Sometimes, there is silence. It is in this place where God is doing an inner work in His children called PERSEVERANCE. You see, when we are looking for the answered prayer, God is looking at our hearts. He wants perseverance to have its perfect work in us so that we can be complete in Him. As we mature in our walk with Him, He does a maturing process that is necessary for growth. He loves us too much to keep us as babes in Christ. This is the love of the Father. Never take His silence as a lack of activity, but trust that He is doing an inner work that in His eyes is more valuable than anything you could ever imagine.

Ask God for the strength to endure His work within you. Then praise Him that He loves you enough to mold you in the image of His Son. Thank Him in advance for the spirit of perseverance that He is producing in you.

Perseverance, My Child

Till the Land

> "Be patient, then, brothers and sisters, until the Lord's coming.
> See how the farmer waits for the land to yield its valuable crop,
> patiently waiting for the autumn and spring rains.
> You too, be patient and stand firm,
> because the Lord's coming is near."
> —James 5:7-8

I MARVEL AT the pristine landscape of farmland. The lush green grass, rolling meadows, and perfectly manicured rows of crops are absolutely breathtaking. What a sight to behold God's creation in its purest form. I often imagine the owners of this farm sitting on the front porch of their farmhouse admiring the beauty of it all. What I don't realize is that farming is one of the most physically demanding occupations to have. What I don't imagine is working outdoors from sunrise to sunset. In order to produce what we see, farmers take on the task of tilling the land. Webster's Dictionary's definition of *till* is: "to labor, as by plowing or harrowing, upon (land) for the raising of crops; cultivate." In order for the rich green grass to grow and the fruits and vegetables to be edible, farmers must labor, plow, and literally break through the soil. Beloved, isn't this what the writer of James admonishes us about? In order for the Lord of heaven to rain down His blessings, we must possess a prayer life that is coupled with patience. We ought to be like the farmer who labors in intense prayer from sunrise to sunset, breaking up any hardness in our hearts, cultivating a heart of worship, and finally creating a clear path for God to plant the seeds of expectancy in our hearts.

While you are persevering in prayer and patiently waiting, know that He will send the rain. Use this prayer time to ask God to till your heart, so that when He speaks, your heart is ready to receive the harvest.

Hidden Treasures

Called to Pray

"I urge, then, first of all, that requests, prayers, intercession and thanksgiving be made for everyone."
—1 Timothy 2:1

NOW MORE THAN ever, we as God's children are called to pray. Unless you are living in seclusion, you are aware of the direction our nation has turned. The world is undergoing trials that even powerful leaders of nations cannot conceive. We are living in perilous times to say the least. Natural disasters seem to be occurring with more frequency than ever before. Thousands upon thousands of men, women, and children are losing their lives in a single day. In the United States of America we say we are a nation under God, but God is being omitted everywhere in our national life. No longer is He present in the schools, courtrooms, or offices—the places where we desperately need Him. Jesus warned His disciples of these times, days of evil. The same warning applies to us today as WE are His disciples in this fallen world. As you lay your requests before God, never forget that we are the light in this dark world, a city on a hill. God's chosen ones should always have a posture of humility and intercede for those who are lost. Remember, Jesus came into the world to seek those who are perishing and to save them; let's follow His lead.

As you pray, pray not only for our nation but also for this world. Ask God for fresh eyes so that you can see His activity and what He is communicating to His children. Remember, He is coming soon and He wants us to be His ambassadors upon this earth.

Called to Pray

The Gift

> "Blessed are those who listen to me,
> watching daily at my doors, waiting at my doorway."
> —Proverbs 8:34

EVERY CHRISTMAS SEASON this is how you can find me: waiting and listening for the sound of a brown truck that is sure to possess what I am waiting for. Unfortunately, I am one of those last-minute online shoppers, so the waiting is filled with a little angst. Yet, online shopping works for me. My procrastination and the waiting is another story. So this is what I do, not wanting to miss the delivery, making sure it ends up on my doorstep not a moment too late. The writer of Proverbs similarly illustrates this concept in relation to obtaining wisdom from God. When we pray, we then should be listening, watching, and waiting for the Lord of heaven and earth to speak. We should be filled with much anticipation that He is on the way with what we have asked of Him—His wisdom. The wisdom

He gives will make us a blessed people. His wisdom is something that we should covet. Anticipating His arrival, longing to hear Him speak, embracing what He shares. To be envied, happy, and fortunate is what being blessed looks like. This is the state we will be in as we pursue the wisdom from on high. I absolutely love the look on the faces of my loved ones as they open the gifts I was anxiously waiting for. Beloved, imagine the look on God's face as we open the gracious gift of wisdom that He has waiting for us…and it's all for the asking!

Ask God to light a fire in you so that He finds you watching, waiting, and listening. Ask Him to give you an excitement for finding and obtaining His wisdom. His wisdom far exceeds any gift we could ever ask for or receive.

Hidden Treasures

Not Guilty

"Let us then approach the throne of grace with confidence,
so that we may receive mercy and find grace to help
us in our time of need."
—Hebrews 4:16

CONDEMNATION, NAGGING DOUBTS, questions of self-worth, and insecurities seem to surround you. Fear grips you and the familiar sense of unease is your everyday existence. Sadly, this is the reality for so many people. When God sent His Son to die for our sins, His death eradicated such a life. We are God's chosen people, a royal priesthood. A people chosen for greatness, as His children, we cannot and should not embrace a life that is contrary to that. On more than one occasion I have encountered many of God's children living in this manner, never once questioning their salvation, but realizing something was amiss. Why do they believe things about themselves that run contrary to God's Word? Who is whispering such hideous lies about them? Whose voice are they listening to? Surely, it's not the voice of Truth. It is the voice of Satan, whose only purpose is to steal, kill, and destroy. His mission is to fill you with lies so that you believe you are not worthy of God's love. He wants nothing more than to deter you from the love of God. Beloved, if you are experiencing life like this, stop! Embrace God's Word and experience the great love He has just for you. Embrace the reality that when He looks at you He sees His Son. He sees the cross. He sees that you have been made righteous through faith. There is nothing that separates you from Him. When you confessed and believed in your heart that He is Lord, God said, "Not guilty!" Beloved, approach His throne of grace and mercy, knowing you are well-loved by the Father. He was rejected so that you would be accepted. He was condemned so that you could have eternal life. Rise up and stand in whom He says you are!

Take time to read His love letter to you and embrace every truth in it. Anything that sets itself against it is from Satan, the father of lies. God is your Father and loves you more than you can ever imagine!

Not Guilty

God of the Living

> "…have you not read what God said to you, 'I am the God of
> Abraham, the God of Isaac, and the God of Jacob'?
> He is not the God of the dead but of the living."
> —Matthew 22:31b-32

AS I READ the awesome stories of Abraham, Isaac, and Jacob, I marvel at the intimacy they shared with God. They walked and talked with God. Sometimes, God told them step by step what to do, and other times they were required to walk by faith with the assurance He was there. God Himself declared that He was their Father. As I was pondering how amazing this must have been, God whispered a truth into my heart that I needed to understand. It was so simple, yet so profound, that while He is the God of Abraham, Isaac, and Jacob, He is my God too. I am alive and well because His Spirit resides within me. He is unchanging. He desires the same intimacy with me. He longs to share with me the mystery of His will for my life.

He wants to walk with me in the valley and when I am soaring above the mountains. He is the God of the living. What we read in His Word is very much alive now. His Word has power now! There is nothing that God did in our forefathers' lives that He cannot and will not do for His children now. What wonderful and exciting news. So often, we forget that the Word of God is for us to know God, to understand who He is. With that heart knowledge, it's time for that knowledge to become our belief. We must walk in it, breathe it, and live it.

Do you believe that now? Are you praying in such a way that reflects your belief in the God of the living? Remember, our forefathers weren't superheroes, they were ordinary people putting their faith in an extraordinary God!

Hidden Treasures

David's Supplication

THE FOLLOWING IS from the heart of a man after God's very own heart. There's such humility and reverence pouring from the heart of David to the Most High God. David stood on the promises of God while trusting in Him with a heart of worship. Please read:

> Then King David went in and sat before the LORD, and he said:
>
> "Who am I, LORD God, and what is my family, that you have brought me this far? And as if this were not enough in your sight, my God, you have spoken about the future of the house of your servant. You, LORD God, have looked on me as though I were the most exalted of men.
>
> "What more can David say to you for honoring your servant? For you know your servant, LORD. For the sake of your

servant and according to your will, you have done this great thing and made known all these great promises.

"There is no one like you, LORD, and there is no God but you, as we have heard with our own ears. And who is like your people Israel—the one nation on earth whose God went out to redeem a people for himself, and to make a name for yourself, and to perform great and awesome wonders by driving out nations from before your people, whom you redeemed from Egypt? You made your people Israel your very own forever, and you, LORD, have become their God.

"And now, LORD, let the promise you have made concerning your servant and his house be established forever. Do as you promised, so that it will be established and that your name will be great forever. Then people will say, 'The LORD Almighty, the God over Israel, is Israel's God!' And the house of your servant David will be established before you.

"You, my God, have revealed to your servant that you will build a house for him. So your servant has found courage to pray to you. You, LORD, are God! You have promised these good things to your servant. Now you have been pleased to bless the house of your servant, that it may continue forever in your sight; for you, LORD, have blessed it, and it will be blessed forever."

—1 Chronicles 17:16-27

In the quietness of your heart and mind, recall the great love that God has shown upon your life. The favor and the blessings of God are immeasurable, thank Him for it!

David's Supplication

Close the Door

*"Submit yourselves, then, to God.
Resist the devil, and he will flee from you."*
—James 4:7

AS WE PRAY, there is a literal war in the spirit realm. The enemy of your soul will use every scheme to distract you from communion with the Father. Remember, he is the father of lies, no truth is found in him. The Gospel of Luke, chapter four, gives us a startling look into this very truth. Jesus, full of the Holy Spirit while in the wilderness fasting and praying, had a visit from Satan himself. Every move the enemy made was used to distract Jesus from His mission upon the earth. Every scripture he quoted was twisted. There was no truth in him. Jesus, in His hungry and exhausted state, fought back with the truth of God's Word. This is the same battle that you and I are in when we seek to draw closer to the Father. You must remain steadfast and immovable in the Word of God. You must pray with an unshakeable faith. This is how you close the door on the enemy of your soul. Remember, the enemy came to steal, kill, and destroy the purpose and destiny of your life. But, Jesus came to give you life and life abundantly. Guard your prayer life with same intensity of your home, car, and earthly possessions. Remember, those things are temporal and can disappear like a mist. But the Word of God is eternal.

When you pray, ask the Father to place a hedge of protection around your thoughts. Ask Him to protect you from the schemes and strategies of the evil one. Ask Him to keep you from temptation. Make it your heart's desire to hide the Word of God in your heart and use it as a weapon to destroy the works of evil.

Hidden Treasures

Pay Attention

"Whether you turn to the right or to the left,
your ears will hear a voice behind you, saying,
'This is the way; walk in it.'"
—Isaiah 30:21

SIGNS WERE EVERYWHERE—a detour sign here, a caution sign there. This is exactly what I encountered as I was traveling on a major highway headed to a conference that I did not want to miss, but boy did I pick the wrong evening. I found myself smack dab in the middle of a construction zone. I have never considered myself one of those drivers who gets flustered, but on that particular evening, I have to admit, I was. It wasn't until I was halfway there that I realized that if I had just slowed down and paid attention to the signs and the changes I was encountering, it wouldn't have been such a nerve-racking trip. So, instead of worrying about my arrival time, I began to drive with the confidence that I would make it there on time, and to my surprise, I did.

Isn't this a reflection of our lives at times? When God is doing a new thing, it catches you off guard if you are not paying attention. Beloved, it doesn't have to be that way. In your walk with Him, He desires intimacy—an intimacy where He can simply whisper in your ear. A place where He can gently warn you of the changes in your life that He planned to take place. He won't shout or force you along the path He has chosen, so it is vital that you allow your soul to be at rest so that you can hear His gentle voice leading and guiding you to the destination that He ordained for you. Keep your eyes focused on Him at all times and trust in His timing.

In your quiet time, ask yourself, am I keeping my eyes on Him, watching for His activity? Am I completely unaware that He is there wanting to be my Shepherd and lead me safely along the path of life?

Pay Attention

Selah

SELAH IN BIBLICAL terms means "to pause, to take a meditative stance upon what you have just read." To calmly think on what you have just taken in. Selah is also defined as a "pregnant" pause. *Pregnant* in the literary sense means "full of meaning or significance, prolific or fruitful." God's Word is living and active. Take time as you read Psalm 46 to fully engage your senses into what the writer is communicating to you in this very moment, in this season of your life. The serenity of this psalm is powerful!

> God is our refuge and strength, an ever-present help in trouble. Therefore we will not fear, though the earth give way and the mountains fall into the heart of the sea, though its waters roar and foam and the mountains quake with their surging. [Selah]
>
> There is a river whose streams make glad the city of God, the holy place where the Most High dwells. God is within her, she will

not fall; God will help her at break of day. Nations are in uproar,
kingdoms fall; he lifts his voice,
the earth melts. The LORD Almighty is with us;
the God of Jacob is our fortress. [Selah]

Come and see what the LORD has done, the desolations he has
brought on the earth. He makes wars cease to the ends of the earth.
He breaks the bow and shatters the spear;
he burns the shields with fire. "Be still,
and know that I am God;
I will be exalted among the nations, I will be exalted in the earth."
The LORD Almighty is with us;
the God of Jacob is our fortress. [Selah]
—Psalm 46

Hidden Treasures

Still the Same

"Jesus Christ is the same yesterday and today and forever."
—Hebrews 13:8

IN PSALM 124:8, the psalmist says, "Our help is in the name of the LORD, the Maker of heaven and earth." When we cry out His name, there is power. His name alone can save. He is the great "I AM." That name alone delivered the Israelites through the raging Red Sea and He is more than able to deliver you. He is El-Shaddai, God Almighty, to those who walk before Him with a pure heart. He is Jehovah–Rohi, our Shepherd who leads and guides all the days of our lives. He is Jehovah–Shammah, ever-present, never leaving or forsaking His children. He is Jehovah-Jireh, providing for His children in their time of need. He is Jehovah-Nissi, our Victory. He fights our battles with victory. He is Jehovah-Shalom, The Lord is Our Peace. The world we live in is ever-changing. From technology to fashion trends, it's hard to keep up with what's hot and what's not. But there is One who never changes. He is the Everlasting God. He is the Eternal Rock, a foundation that can never be shaken or moved. You can stand on the promises of God forever. He is not like man, who can lie. He is Jehovah-Yahweh, our divine salvation. He is the very foundation on which we will stand, now and forevermore. Beloved, when your life seems to spin out of control, bow before the One who is there always, never changing, and ready for you to find rest in Him and Him alone.

Simply thank God for who He is!

Still the Same

A Hope that Unfolds

> "And hope does not put us to shame, because
> God's love has been poured out into our hearts through
> the Holy Spirit, who has been given to us."
> —Romans 5:5

WHEN YOU ARE in prayer with the Almighty, something amazing is taking place in the heavens. Something amazing also begins to unfold inside of you. As you pray with faith, God begins to breathe new life into you. Light begins to penetrate those dark places. As you pray with an uncompromising trust, hope springs forth. That hope brings with it a joy and peace that is indescribable. This is the hope that the Father has called you to. A hope that builds with expectation every time you bow before the throne. Beloved, don't miss out on experiencing this hope that is so freely given. Remember, we have the Holy Spirit living in us. He is our helper; what we cannot do on our own, He is more than able to accomplish in and through us. Allow His Spirit to penetrate so deeply that the eternal hope that God in His love predestined for you to have will pour out until it overflows. He promises that those who put their hope in Him will never be ashamed or disappointed. (See Romans 10:9-11.) I don't know about you, but I want to experience this overflow of hope. Why not begin today?

Take a note of the changes stirring in your heart as you praise and worship the Father. Allow your senses to be dulled. Quiet your soul and allow His Spirit to have its way within you. Never underestimate the power of the hope that begins to arise in you; it will transform you from the inside out!

Hidden Treasures

The Wait Is Over

> "And a woman was there who had been subject to bleeding for twelve years, but no one could heal her. She came up behind him and touched the edge of his cloak, and immediately her bleeding stopped."
> —Luke 8:43-44

COULD YOU IMAGINE a life plagued with chronic bleeding ravaging every part of your body? Could you imagine exhausting every avenue for a cure? Could you imagine carrying the weight of disappointment as even the wisest physicians could not find a cure for what ails you? As I read the account of this dear woman found in the eighth chapter of Luke, I am reminded of what never giving up looks like. She spent her life savings searching for ways to end the agony she endured for twelve years—a life spent sick and unable to live a "normal" life. I imagine when all human effort amounted to nothing, there was a glimmer of hope that was still shining. In a display of faith mixed with desperation she spots the One she has heard could heal on a crowded street. She pushes her frail body through the crowd. At last, she manages to touch the edge of His cloak. Unbeknownst to her, this encounter with the Healer would change her life forever. Her time had finally come; the wait was over. You see, God has time in His hands. He knows just how long to keep you, even in the midst of insurmountable circumstances. He has a set time for your healing. Nothing is by coincidence with God; He knew this woman's time had come. He knew she would step out in faith and have a hope that ultimately led to her healing. When you are tempted to give up, remember this woman. Her hope was alive when everything she tried failed her. Trust that God has not forgotten. He sees and He knows. There is an expiration date on the season that you are in and the wait will finally be over.

As you pray, know that He has the power to heal what ails you—spiritually, physically, emotionally. He is able to heal. Thank Him in advance for this awesome power.

The Wait Is Over

The Promise

> "My comfort in my suffering is this:
> Your promise preserves my life."
> —Psalm 119:50

HAVE YOU EVER received a vision or dream from God? Oh, what joy and excitement it is when the God of the universe shares a glimpse of the plans He has for you. But what happens next may surprise you, something that most of us wouldn't necessarily ask for. What follows is often characterized as a season of testing, adversity, and suffering. You see, God in His awesome splendor has great plans for your life, and because He is your Creator He knows you inside and out. He is well aware of your every move, thought, and motive behind your actions. He wants to make sure that what He intends to bring about, you are ready to receive. You have to be able to handle what He is about to put into your hands.

Unlike us, He is not worried about time. He is looking at our hearts, our character, and our faith in Him. It is often during this time of testing that we question Him. We question if we actually heard from Him, we question His love, we question everything we thought we knew. It is in this time that He is building our faith. It is in this time that His love is more real than ever. It is in this time you must arm yourself with the Word of God, fervently pray, and stand on His rich promise that He will never leave you nor forsake you.

Beloved, it is He who gives dreams and visions. He is the Good Shepherd that speaks clearly to His children. What He does in the meantime is only what a loving Father ought to do. He is preparing you for what is to come. He is building your spiritual muscles. He is building into you the virtues of patience, perseverance, love, joy, peace, kindness, goodness, faithfulness, gentleness, self-control, and a greater intimacy with Him. Trust Him during this time and know that His promises concerning you are "Yes and Amen in Christ Jesus." (See 2 Corinthians 1:20.)

Thank God that He is the dream-giver, that He loves you and wants the best for your life. Thank Him for holding your hand through every season of your life.

Hidden Treasures

Suddenly

> "About midnight Paul and Silas were praying and singing hymns to God, and the other prisoners were listening to them. Suddenly there was such a violent earthquake that the foundations of the prison were shaken. At once all the prison doors flew open, and everyone's chains came loose."
> —Acts 16:25-26

STRIPPED, BEATEN, AND imprisoned. This was now the way of life for the faithful followers of Jesus Christ—a life of submission to God, a life of persecution from the world. One truth remained: they had seen the Messiah. They walked and talked with Him and believed He was who He said He was. They believed that when they left this earth they would see Him again in heaven for all eternity. This reality is what set them in motion to spread the gospel at all costs. Imprisonment to them was no surprise; it was a way of life. Even in the midst of the abuse they encountered they lived a life of praise unto the risen

Messiah. In the midnight hour, sitting in a prison cell, voices filled the air. These voices were crying out to God, crying out to God with hymns of praise and thanksgiving. You see, they knew the Messiah from experience. They knew their mission. They knew that the life they were living was no longer their own. They knew that in all things, the King of Kings was to be glorified. He was the only One who could deliver, if He chose to do so. So, from a pure heart, worship came through those prison walls and as the praise reached the heavens, God shook the earth and miraculously loosed the chains of Paul and Silas, His faithful ones. They were free!

God says that He dwells in the praises of His people. Never allow the circumstances of your life to dull your affection to the One who can deliver. Don't wallow in your "prison"—instead, use this season to become a true worshipper and watch the God of all creation shake the foundation of your circumstance. He hears the cry of His people. He is a God of deliverance and restoration. Watch and be amazed!

Suddenly

A Place of Rest

"Before they call I will answer;
while they are still speaking I will hear."
—Isaiah 65:24

IT IS ALWAYS a comfort to be in the presence of someone who "knows" you. There are people you meet who you instantly connect with in a way that, humanly speaking, cannot be explained. A place where words may not be spoken but you can simply just rest in that person's company, a relationship where you can be your authentic self. This is how I view my prayer life with the Father. Without leaving the comfort of my home, I can kneel before the Father and have an "instant connection." With so many things swirling in my mind and heart, sometimes I am unsure of what to pray for, but He knows. Then I remember that all of my days were ordained, that He knows the very number of hairs upon my head. He knows what burdens I carry and the weight of it all. He knows the path I take and every emotion that comes along with it. He formed me in my mother's womb and knows my thoughts before I even think them. When I finally find the words to communicate to God, He has already heard and is waiting with open arms with an answer!

Ah, the joy that fills my heart to know that God loves me in such an intimate way. Before I pray, He hears. What He wants to do is to quiet my soul and for me to enter into His rest.

Beloved, when you cannot find the words and when you struggle with being still before Him, please embrace this truth.

Hidden Treasures

Hall of Faith

INDUCTION INTO THE Pro Football Hall of Fame is considered to be the NFL's highest honor given to those who have made significant contributions to professional football. The men selected are viewed as leaders both on and off the field and are honored by their peers for their faithfulness on the playing field. In the book of Hebrews, we are introduced to an elite group of individuals who had one thing in common—faith. They have now become known as the Bible's Hall of Faith. Take time to read the whole chapter and witness firsthand how God's chosen people put their faith into action.

Here are just a few:

> "By faith Noah, when warned about things not yet seen, in holy fear built an ark to save his family. By his faith he condemned the world and became heir of the righteousness that is in keeping with faith."
>
> —Hebrews 11:7

"By faith Abraham, when called to go to a place he would later receive as his inheritance, obeyed and went, even though he did not know where he was going."
—Hebrews 11:8

"And by faith even Sarah, who was past childbearing age, was enabled to bear children because she considered him faithful who had made the promise."
—Hebrews 11:11

"By faith Abraham, when God tested him, offered Isaac as a sacrifice. He who had embraced the promises was about to sacrifice his one and only son, even though God had said to him, 'It is through Isaac that your offspring will be reckoned.' Abraham reasoned that God could even raise the dead, and so in a manner of speaking he did receive Isaac back from death."
—Hebrews 11:17-19

"By faith the people passed through the Red Sea as on dry land; but when the Egyptians tried to do so, they were drowned."
—Hebrews 11:29

"By faith the walls of Jericho fell, after the army had marched around them for seven days.
—Hebrews 11:30

Hall of Faith

The Unexpected

*"Keep on loving one another as brothers and sisters.
Do not forget to show hospitality to strangers,
for by so doing some people have shown hospitality
to angels without knowing it."*
—Hebrews 13:1-2

SOMETIMES ANSWERS TO our prayers arrive in unexpected ways. Sometimes answers to our prayers come as a result of extending kindness to others, not realizing that the blessing is wrapped in our kindness to others. I will never forget the day when as a mother of three children, I was having one of those exhaustion-filled days. As I was fixing lunch, I began to pray. It was one of those prayers where I simply said to God that I was tired and was ready for naptime to come and come quickly. I needed a break and I wanted God to give me one. Not more than five minutes had passed when the doorbell rang. It was a neighbor who stopped by to chat for a little while.

In my mind, this was not the greatest time, but I invited her in and we talked while the kids were eating. As the kids were finishing up, my precious neighbor began to clean the table off, help my youngest out of his seat, put dishes in the dishwasher and even entertained the kids while I cleaned up the kitchen. By the time her visit was over, the kids were ready for a nap! As I closed the door, I realized God in His great love for me sent His angel over on assignment just for me. By opening the door of my home and not wallowing in my crazy moment, I invited God's answer to my prayer into my home. God works in ways you could never imagine. Never underestimate how He moves and who He uses to bless you.

As you pray, ask God to enlighten your spiritual eyes and ears to His movement and His voice. Then, be open to how He answers your prayers and remember that His thoughts and ways are so much higher than our own.

Hidden Treasures

He Knows

"Who can fathom the Spirit of the Lord,
or instruct the Lord as his counselor?"
—Isaiah 40:13

"Why do you complain, Jacob? Why do you say, Israel, 'My way is hidden from the Lord; my cause is disregarded by my God?' Do you not know? Have you not heard? The Lord is the everlasting God, the Creator of the ends of the earth. He will not grow tired or weary, and his understanding no one can fathom."

—Isaiah 40:27-28

MY FRIEND, HAVE you ever been in prayer before the Father with a heaviness that you cannot explain? A place where words seem to fail you? A place where you know with all of your heart that your Saviour is waiting with open arms, but you don't have the strength to move? You feel as though your way is hidden from the Creator of the universe. You feel as if the season you are in has lasted just a little too long. I confess that I have been there and it is in this very place where I am reminded that nothing can separate me from the Father's love, that He is surrounding me even if I can't see. He reminds me that He is in control even when I feel that my life is out of order. He gently whispers that He understands the emotions that seem to overwhelm me. It is in this place where prayer beckons me to draw closer to an all-knowing God, a God whose wisdom I cannot comprehend. Beloved, this is one of the many wonders of prayer. We serve a God who sees all things. In this life, we face situations that are beyond our understanding. Stand on the promise that His Word contains all that we need to live this life.

Prayer allows us to cry out to Him, bringing with us all that concerns us and leaving it there. Resting in a complete assurance that He sees, He hears, He understands and He knows.

He Knows

Finding Truth, Walking in Freedom

"But when he, the Spirit of truth, comes, he will guide you
into all the truth. He will not speak on his own;
he will speak only what he hears,
and he will tell you what is yet to come."
—John 16:13

GOD IS HOLY. Everything about Him is righteous and perfect. In His grace and mercy, He has adopted us into His family as beloved children. What was done through His Son on the cross paid the price for our sins, now and forever. With this wonderful truth in mind, are there times in your prayer life where an unsettling silence exists, when it seems He does not hear? You then wonder how a loving God can seem to ignore the cries of His precious children. Beloved, please understand that God is passionate for you. He wants nothing more than to be in sweet fellowship with you. There is nothing that He would not do for His children, but He is Holy. Isaiah 59:2 reminds us,

"But your iniquities have separated you from your God; your sins have hidden his face from you, so that he will not hear." Where there is unconfessed sin, the Holy Spirit within you is grieved. What God desires in that very moment is repentance and a chance to communicate His truths to you about your heart. This is the where the precious gift of the Holy Spirit comes into play. The Holy Spirit's role is to guide you into the wondrous truths of God. It is in this place where you are enlightened to the true condition of your heart and to a restored fellowship with God. A place where the Holy Spirit then gives you the power to walk in that truth and experience a life-giving freedom like never before. The power and the faith to know that when you pray, nothing is separating you from the Father. You and the Father are now one…how awesome is that!

As you enter into quiet time with the Father, say this prayer:

"Search me, God, and know my heart; test me and know my anxious thoughts. See if there is any offensive way in me, and lead me in the way everlasting."
—Psalm 139:23-24

Hidden Treasures

The Rolling Away

"Then the LORD said to Joshua, 'Today I have rolled away the reproach of Egypt from you.' So the place has been called Gilgal to this day."
—Joshua 5:9

IN THE BOOK of Joshua we are introduced to a mighty man of valor. A new season was upon the Israelites as they had mourned the death of Moses for thirty days and now Joshua was their leader. After wandering in the wilderness for forty years, now was the time to cross over into the Promised Land. It was a new beginning, a place where the land was flowing with milk and honey. God, in His timing, arranged it so that before conquering the land, they would have to pass through Gilgal. In Hebrew, Gilgal sounds like *gilal*, which means "to roll." Here at Gilgal, they lived and worshipped. It was their commanding base as they were arming themselves for the conquest of the land. In preparation for this new undertaking, the Lord then commanded

Joshua to go throughout the camp and make the Israelites a circumcised people again, a symbol of renewal. God wanted the hearts of this new generation totally committed to Him. He wanted them "to roll away" old mindsets and embrace the new life being offered. The old generation of Israelites perished in the wilderness because of their disobedience, causing them to never enter into the promise. With boldness, Joshua did as he was commanded and circumcised the men, symbolizing the progression of cutting away an old way of life and the beginning of a new one. This covenant represented the reproach of slavery in Egypt being rolled away. Now the memory was gone forever and their sights set on the Promised Land. What does God need to cut away in your life? What healing needs to take place? What can God roll away from your life before He brings you into your promised land?

As you seek Him in prayer, lay this before Him so that when you enter into the place He has designed for your life, you will do so with the reproach of your past rolled away and a completeness in Christ that will blow your mind!

The Rolling Away

Ordinary Man, Extraordinary Prayer

"Jabez was more honorable than his brothers. His mother had
named him Jabez, saying, 'I gave birth to him in pain.'
Jabez cried out to the God of Israel, 'Oh, that you would bless me
and enlarge my territory! Let your hand be with me,
and keep me from harm so that I will be free from pain.'
And God granted his request."
—1 Chronicles 4:9-10

HAVE YOU EVER wanted God to bless you beyond your wildest dreams? A chance to experience life and life abundantly on this side of eternity? A chance to live in God's perfect will? To be in complete agreement with all that the Father says about you in His Holy Word? Even as I write this, it brings such excitement to my heart because this is what I want! I want to see His hand upon me, moving mountains out of my way as I run to the destiny He has for me. I want to be in a place where I am blessed so much that I am full—a fullness that then manifests itself into blessings poured over into the lives of others. I want to escape my "four-walled" existence that I have created and live in God's landscape, a horizon filled with endless possibilities. I want to see and feel a hedge of protection around me so that I am safe in the arms of the Mighty One.

What about you? Do you want God's very best? An ordinary man by the name Jabez did, and he had the audacity to ask for it and God had the audacity to grant him his request. Beloved, you are Jabez and because God is unchanging, His answer will be the same for you.

Find a quiet place where you have the time to read and meditate on these two verses. Allow them to have a place in your heart and pray them to the Father until they become your very own words.

Hidden Treasures

A Cry in the Night

"I cried out to God for help;
I cried out to God to hear me.
When I was in distress, I sought the Lord;
at night I stretched out untiring hands,
and I would not be comforted.
I remembered you, God, and I groaned;
I meditated, and my spirit grew faint.
You kept my eyes from closing;
I was too troubled to speak.
I thought about the former days,
the years of long ago;
I remembered my songs in the night.
My heart meditated and my spirit asked:
'Will the Lord reject forever?
Will he never show his favor again?
Has his unfailing love vanished forever?

> Has his promise failed for all time?
> Has God forgotten to be merciful?
> Has He in anger withheld his compassion?'"
> —Psalm 77:1-9

I REMEMBER A season in my life when I could not form the words to pray. Depression was all around me. A cloud of darkness loomed over me like a heavy blanket. There were days when I couldn't see my way from one moment to the next. It was literally a time when I was going from strength to strength. The joy of the Lord was truly my only source of strength. It was in this time that I discovered Psalm 77, a heartfelt cry to the One who can save, the One who sees, and the One who can restore. Beloved, sometimes this is what your prayer life will look like and that's okay. Jesus promised that in this life we would have troubles, but to take heart because on the cross He overcame. So, in the midst of a valley moment, don't be afraid to pour out your heart to Him and trust that He hears and that He will answer you in your time of need.

In your quiet time, set aside some time to read and meditate on the following passage. In the next section we will see the faithfulness of God in the second half of this psalm.

A Cry in the Night

A Declaration of His Faithfulness

As you are before the Lord in prayer, reflect on this passage:

"Then I thought, 'To this I will appeal:
the years when the Most High stretched out his right hand.
I will remember the deeds of the LORD;
yes, I will remember your miracles of long ago.
I will consider all your works
and meditate on all your mighty deeds.'
Your ways, God, are holy.
What god is as great as our God?
You are the God who performs miracles;
you display your power among the peoples.
With your mighty arm you redeemed your people,
the descendants of Jacob and Joseph.
The waters saw you, God,
the waters saw you and writhed;
the very depths were convulsed.
The clouds poured down water,

A Declaration of His Faithfulness

> the heavens resounded with thunder;
> your arrows flashed back and forth.
> Your thunder was heard in the whirlwind,
> your lightning lit up the world;
> the earth trembled and quaked.
> Your path led through the sea,
> your way through the mighty waters,
> though your footprints were not seen.
> You led your people like a flock
> by the hand of Moses and Aaron."
> —Psalm 77:10-20

LAST SECTION WE talked about a season of life that is marked with difficulties. A season in which depression tries to rob you of the joy and peace rendered to you by the Most High God. We then looked at the first half of Psalm 77 and found comfort that the psalmist had the courage to cry out to God when all seemed lost. Today, we will look at the second half of the psalm and we are now witnessing a change. Not a change in the circumstance, but a change in perspective. The psalmist begins to declare with confidence the faithfulness of God. This is where the darkness begins to break, where a silver lining appears on those luminous clouds that hang overhead. This is where we begin to experience a breakthrough in our own prayer life. We have poured out our hearts to God, but now we must take the magnifying glass off our trial and magnify the One who has the power to remove the season. He loves to hear the praises of His people, even in the midst of a valley. Magnify Him, exalt Him, and remember His great love for you. As you praise, He will gently take you by the hand and lead you out of the valley to your mountaintop. Begin declaring who God is and watch Him move!

Hidden Treasures

An Inexpressible Joy

"Though you have not seen him, you love him;
and even though you do not see him now,
you believe in him and are filled with an
inexpressible and glorious joy."
—1 Peter 1:8

THERE ARE MOMENTS in life that bring such happiness to the human heart. The birth of my children, watching them take their first steps, and hearing their first words are memories that will be forever etched in my heart. Of course, life presents us with challenges. Those moments in life when happiness is nowhere to be found, the death of a loved one, the loss of a job, a health crisis. Each of these real-life scenarios has the ability to bring about a wide array of emotions, from anger, sadness, frustration, etc. You may have had to face a few trials in life that could have had the potential to break you. But what a blessing it is to be a child of God, because in the midst of trying times and the emotions that accompany them, something happens within that I can only describe as supernatural. You see, in these times as you and I press into the Father, His Holy Spirit begins to work. That work then produces joy. Joy is not dependent upon circumstances. Joy is something that catches you by surprise, even surprising others as they watch you go through a difficult season. Joy is a deep, soul-satisfying feeling that comes from above, because it defies any human thoughts or feelings. Psalm 30:5 reminds us that "weeping may stay for the night, but rejoicing comes in the morning." This happens by pressing into God and allowing the Holy Spirit to produce a joy in you that frees you to praise Him despite what you are facing. When you pray, allow the joy of knowing the Lord your God, believing in the Lord your God, and hoping in the Lord your God to be your strength, now and forevermore!

An Inexpressible Joy

Living in Obedience and Blessed

> "If you are willing and obedient,
> you will eat the good things of the land."
> —Isaiah 1:19

ONE OF MY most treasured and rewarding moments of prayer is hearing from God. It is in my quiet time with the Father that He gives instructions, encouragement, and sometimes rebuke. Through the power of the Holy Spirit, God is expecting me to respond to Him in complete obedience. There should never be a time when I hear from Him and not respond accordingly, since James 1:23-24 says: "Anyone who listens to the word but does not do what it says is like someone who looks at his face in a mirror and, after looking at himself, goes away and immediately forgets what he looks like." Basically, it's allowing God's word to go in one ear and out the other. Doesn't make sense, does it? But so often this is what we as His children do. How unfortunate it is to miss the blessings of God because we

Living in Obedience and Blessed

fail to respond in obedience. God promises that if we respond to His voice we will be a blessed people. He promises to pour so many blessings on you that you cannot contain them. He promises that no matter where you make your home, you'll be blessed. He promises that your children will be blessed, even your animals! He promises to set you apart as His child, holy unto Himself. He promises to open the windows of heaven and cause rain to come in due season. He promises to make you the head and not the tail. You will walk with the authority of Jesus Christ.

Whew! Those blessings are the blessings that no man can give nor take away. We serve a powerful God, who is holding all of creation in the palm of His mighty hand. When He speaks, listen and obey.

As you pray, make sure the communication is two-way. Never talk so much that His voice is drowned out. Take some time to hear Him. Allow His voice to drown out all others. Pour out your heart before the King, but never leave your quiet time with your heart empty; allow Him to fill it with His words.

Hidden Treasures

Wandering in Disobedience and Cursed

> "But if you resist and rebel,
> you will be devoured by the sword.
> For the mouth of the LORD has spoken."
> —Isaiah 1:20

LAST SECTION WE saw how God showers blessings upon us as we respond in obedience to Him. Now, let's talk about what the opposite looks like. If we are honest with ourselves, we know that there are or have been areas of disobedience in our lives. Not a comfortable place to be, yet, in His rich grace and mercy, He still gives us an opportunity to repent and go the way He is commanding. The Word of God reminds us that whatever we sow, that shall we reap. If we sow to the flesh and disobedience, we will reap discipline from a Father who loves us too much to allow us to keep running from Him. God says that He will not be mocked, so when we go against Him there are consequences. He warns us that curses will come down hard upon us. He warns us that whatever we put our hands to, it will not prosper. He warns us that whether we come or go, we will be oppressed. He warns us that He will send a cloud of confusion upon our heads because we persist in our own way. He warns that the enemy of our souls will attack us hard and we will be defeated. Beloved, please know that God your God loves you with an everlasting love. In His great love, He sent His Son for the atonement of our sins. There is no greater love. He wants to enjoy sweet fellowship with you. He wants to make life sweet, but He is holy and we are to worship Him with a holy and reverent awe. When He speaks, listen.

Let's not take advantage of His kindness and longsuffering towards us, but let's choose to walk the path of obedience in response to His great love for us. Pray for a heart that is truly submitted to Him and His ways. Where there is disobedience, repent and embrace the path of obedience and the blessings that follow it.

Wandering in Disobedience and Cursed

Rejoice!

> "In all this you greatly rejoice, though now for a little while you may have had to suffer grief in all kinds of trials. These have come so that the proven genuineness of your faith—of greater worth than gold, which perishes even though refined by fire—may result in praise, glory and honor when Jesus Christ is revealed."
> —1 Peter 1:6-7

IN THIS LIFE we are going to face hardships of every kind. There will be seasons of difficulties that we must endure. In the midst of these times it is comforting to know that there is a God who is in control. Unlike us, God sees our lives from a different perspective, one that is higher than ours. He has an eternal view, one that puts to death our limited human wisdom. I remember sitting on a plane headed to sunny Florida and looking down below at the landscape. It truly amazed me at just how perfect everything looked from on high. The land looked totally

Rejoice!

different than what we see in our everyday existence. We take for granted that every part of the land is carefully grafted and plotted. The perfect order of squares, rectangles and carefully put together subdivisions gave me a different view of the land we live in. Beloved, that's how God sees our lives: intricately knit together for a purpose that we cannot yet see. Even the messy part of our lives, even the trials that seem to take us under, while we see in them a jumbled mess, He sees a masterpiece being put together by His design. This is why He says to rejoice when we face various trials, trusting that He is doing an invaluable work in us that only He can do. He is carefully refining us into something more precious and valuable than we could ever envision for ourselves. When gold is heated, the impurities rise to the surface and are taken away so that only the purest of gold remains. When we go through the fire, we are naked before our King and He will take away all that is not of Him. We will be refined, tested, tried, and ready for the purpose to which He has called us. Take heart and know that He who started this work in you will not finish until you are made complete in Christ Jesus…and this, my friend, is why we rejoice!

Spend time in prayer and thank God for the trials of this life. Thank Him for being in control even when cannot see the whole picture. Finally, thank Him for having a perfect design for our lives.

Hidden Treasures

Life

"The mind governed by the flesh is death,
but the mind governed by the Spirit is life and peace."
—Romans 8:6

WHAT A GIFT God the Father has given us with the presence of the Holy Spirit in our lives. What a blessing to know that when we pray, He who dwells within us already knows what is going on in our lives. This is why, when we pray, it is the time to leave our human wisdom behind, casting down every thought that sets itself against the awesome wisdom of God. To allow ourselves to be immersed in the fullness of who God is. There have been many times when I have entered into prayer with burdens that are far too heavy to carry already thinking of solutions and even possible outcomes. But this is not what He desires. He desires for us to have a heart of submission to the life-giving power of the Holy Spirit. This awesome power brings peace and wisdom that surpasses our own. This awesome power takes a firm grip on our flesh and removes us from the path of spiritual death. He desires for us to give our feelings to Him and allow the Spirit to mold, reshape, and sometimes discard. When we stay in our flesh without allowing the Holy Spirit to permeate our prayer time, we never see what God wants us to see. We miss hearing from God and what He has to say. It breaks His heart for us not to experience the richness and fullness of true fellowship with the Father. Remember, He knows the way that we take, He understands the emotions that surround us even before we pray, but He welcomes us to come unto Him and He will give us rest. That means laying aside all that concerns us, submitting our flesh to His lordship, and allowing the Holy Spirit to have His way. Living a life ruled by emotions always leads to death, but living a life controlled by the Holy Spirit leads to life and life abundantly!

When you pray, remember that God wants you to have a peace that passes all understanding and an uninhibited trust in Him. You can surrender it all knowing that He longs to take care of you and lead you to true life found only in Him.

Life

Are You Willing to Wait?

"There was also a prophet, Anna, the daughter of Penuel, of the tribe of Asher. She was very old; she had lived with her husband seven years after her marriage, and then was a widow for eighty-four years. She never left the temple but worshiped night and day, fasting and praying. Coming up to them at that very moment, she gave thanks to God and spoke about the child to all who were looking forward to the redemption of Jerusalem."
—Luke 2:36-38

THE STORY OF Anna the prophetess is one of the most profound examples of waiting in the Bible. Oftentimes, it is overlooked because it is wrapped in the middle of the miraculous account of our Savior's birth. However, hers is a story filled with hope. Anna was only married for a total of seven years before she became a widow, eighty-four years have since passed and now her hope begins to unfold. She spent her days and nights worshipping in the temple, fasting, and praying to God. She had a unique closeness to God and knew the time for the prophetic fulfillment of the Messiah would soon come to pass. She never lost hope that she would one day behold the Messiah. What a testament of what it means to worship while you are waiting! What a steadfastness in prayer and faithfulness unto God! What a joy she must have felt when, just at the right time, she walked into the temple as Mary and Joseph were presenting the Messiah, baby Jesus, to the priests. God, in His rich love for Anna, allowed her to participate in this wondrous event. Her years on this earth were marked by a dedication of her mind, body, and soul unto the Lord, all leading to this blessed event.

Beloved, are you willing to wait it out? Whatever you are believing God for, know that He has it. He has already ordained the days of your life, down to the most intricate details. Never give up praying, fasting, and believing. Never lose the hope that the Holy Spirit infuses you with each time you pray. Know that just like Anna, you will behold the promises He has for you!

Hidden Treasures

A Light Shining in Darkness

"And God said, "Let there be lights in the vault of the sky to separate the day from the night, and let them serve as signs to mark seasons, and days and years."
—Genesis 1:14

IN THE BEGINNING, God created the sun, moon, and stars to shine upon all of creation. In the beginning, God decided to separate day from night, bringing light in dark places. In the beginning God, showcasing His providence, set the seasons in place to bring His divine order upon the earth. This is what prayer accomplishes in our relationship with Him. Because He is sovereign, He creates circumstances just so that His glory can be seen. By the Word of God, the Holy Spirit illuminates truth into the most innermost parts of your heart. His very Word sheds light on any situation that you may find yourself in. God, in His care for you, ordains the seasons of your life so that you will seek Him and thereby find Him. In seasons of sadness, depression, or spiritual apathy, He possesses the power to shine His love upon you. Psalm 139:12 reminds us, "Even the darkness will not be dark to you; the night will shine like the day, for darkness is as light to you." Even in the darkest season of your life, He is there, shining His light upon you. His Word leads you into truth, as a lamp unto your feet, shining brightly on the path that is set before you. Beloved, rest assured that this is why prayer is so powerful. In our limited knowledge, He has every answer. He is a Father who is willing and ready to show you truth. He cries out to us passionately, "I have come into the world as a light, so that no one who believes in me should stay in darkness" (John 12:46).

In your quiet time, enter in cleaving to these truths, trusting in Him and relying on Him to shine light in those areas where there is darkness...He will do it!

A Light Shining in Darkness

The Discipline of Fasting

> "And He said to them, 'This kind cannot be driven out by anything but prayer and fasting.'"
> —Mark 9:29 NKJV

IN THE GOSPEL of Mark in chapter nine, we witness a father's desperate plea for the healing hands of Jesus to touch his demon-possessed son. As the man approaches Jesus, he explains the severity of his son's condition. This young boy was living in constant terror as a result; so was his father. The demon inside him had taken over, causing him to go into fits of convulsions, foaming at the mouth and grinding his teeth. What possessed him was far too strong to be contained in the body of a young boy. The father then explained that when he asked Jesus's own disciples, they couldn't drive the demonic spirit out. Now, here he was, standing before Jehovah-Rapha hoping for a miracle. And a miracle he received. Not only was the boy delivered from the evil spirit, but the father's faith was revitalized, all by the

The Discipline of Fasting

asking. Here is where the lesson comes in. After witnessing all of this, the disciples in their angst asked Jesus why they couldn't perform this miracle when Jesus had given them the authority to drive out impure spirits and to heal every disease and sickness. So, you can imagine their surprise when Jesus simply said, "This kind cannot be driven out by anything but prayer and fasting." So simple, yet very profound. Fasting not only denies the body of food, but it is a discipline of self-denial that is at work. Fasting allows your flesh to be crucified and the Holy Spirit within you is allowed to have complete reign over your thinking, doing, and being. It is in this realm that God's power can come through with such force that you cannot deny His presence. So powerful that there is no room for self-exaltation, realizing that only God can do what He does in and through you when you fast. This was a humbling lesson for the disciples as it is for us today. There will be a time when total reliance on God will call you to this spiritual discipline. As you empty yourself of earthly pleasures, He promises to fill you with eternal pleasures that will cause an overflow of faith and power that only God can give!

If you have never practiced the discipline of fasting, approach His throne and ask Him how. He will show you how and when. He says in His word that if anyone asks for His wisdom, He will freely give without faultfinding.

Hidden Treasures

Secret Place

"But when you pray, go into your room, close the door
and pray to your Father, who is unseen. Then your Father,
who sees what is done in secret, will reward you."
—Matthew 6:6

THERE IS A place that I absolutely love to visit, a secret place. A place where I can be with God and He can be with me and mold me into the woman that He already sees that I am. A place where I am free to be completely me, flaws and all. A quiet, secluded place where no one else is there but my Father in heaven and me. There is no pressure to say the right words: I simply say what's on my heart because He already knows. When I cannot find the words to communicate, sitting in silence is totally acceptable. Sometimes in that silence, a praise will emanate from my soul and glorify the One to whom I am praying. In this secret place I begin to feel His presence, an experience that I treasure and yearn to be in always. In this place, His grace and mercy surround me as I lay all of my burdens at His feet. This is what He wants all of His children to experience. Trust that when you make it your soul's desire to be in this place, He sees and He rewards those who seek Him. What you do in secret brings glory to the Father and He will reward you openly. Beloved, when Jesus walked this earth, He, too, often went to a quiet, secluded place to pray, a secret place. We must do the same.

As a woman, I know that there are seasons of life where the morning hours can be unpredictable, especially with young children. Don't become legalistic in your thinking towards prayer. Instead, ask God for wisdom in when and where to pray in a secret place. He delights in His children when they seek wisdom and He will show you!

Secret Place

Rules of the Game

> "But the Advocate, the Holy Spirit, whom the Father will send in my name, will teach you all things and will remind you of everything I have said to you."
> —John 14:26

SURPRISINGLY, OVER THE years, I have come to like football. While I stake no claim to a particular team and am far from being a football fanatic, I do enjoy watching a good game. At the heart of every game is the field general, otherwise known as the quarterback. The quarterback essentially leads, directing the team on game day. It is vital to the health of the team that the quarterback studies the playbook and sets plays that will lead the team to victory. It wasn't until recently that I discovered something that blew my mind. Inside the helmet of the quarterback is a small speaker in each earhole that allows him to directly hear from coaches off the field, reminding him of plays or instructing him on changes that need to be made according to how the game is unfolding. There is no need for excessive time-outs to communicate, therefore allowing the game to be played and the quarterback the freedom to listen, respond, and make the play. Beloved, we have a "speaker" who gives us play-by-play direction for our lives daily. Before Jesus left this earth, He promised the Holy Spirit would be sent in His name to indwell us forever. The Holy Spirit is our intercessor, helper, strengthener, advocate, and counselor. Whenever we are facing a season of uncertainty, the Holy Spirit, like those coaches on the sideline, causes us to remember all that the Father has taught us. When life begins to change, the Holy Spirit instructs us and leads the way. What an awesome thing to know that in this game of life we are never alone!

In your prayer time, take time to thank God for the precious gift of the Holy Spirit and the awesome gifts that He brings!

Hidden Treasures

Pass It On

"They replied, 'Believe in the Lord Jesus, and you will be saved—you and your household. Then they spoke the word of the Lord to him and to all the others in his house.'"
—Acts 16:31-32

AFTER BEING STRIPPED and beaten, Paul and Silas were then placed in shackles, imprisoned because they persisted in preaching the gospel of Jesus Christ at all cost. Late in the midnight hour while they were praising God, the earth began to tremble causing the shackles they were chained by to come loose. God from on high looked down upon His servants and delivered them from their imprisonment. Oh, but the story does not end there. Trembling with fear at what he had just witnessed, the jailer in charge was intent on taking his own life because he would be held responsible for what appeared to be an escape. Refusing to take their freedom and run, Paul and Silas saw this opportunity to further expand the kingdom of God. All in one hour, look at what took place:

> "At that hour of the night the jailer took them and washed their wounds; then immediately he and all his household were baptized. The jailer brought them into his house and set a meal before them; he was filled with joy because he had come to believe in God—he and his whole household."
> —Acts 16:33-34

What an awesome privilege we have as His children to share with others the goodness and faithfulness of a God who can and will do the miraculous in our lives. The jailer saw firsthand the splendor of God and then received the best gift of all, salvation. Not just for himself but for his family as well. This is why we are commanded to make disciples while we are here on this earth. What a shame it would be for us to keep this treasure to ourselves. Beloved, we were chosen to be His children, but there are so many who are lost. Once you have received Him, you have to pass it on so that the great commission is fulfilled to the ends of the earth.

Take some time in prayer and ask God how He can use you to reach the lost. Ask Him to lay those lost sheep upon your heart who are desperately in need of a Shepherd.

Pass It On

The Voice

> "The voice of the LORD is powerful;
> the voice of the LORD is majestic.
> The voice of the LORD breaks the cedars;
> the LORD breaks in pieces the cedars of Lebanon."
> —Psalm 29:4-5

THE CEDARS OF Lebanon are enormous trees that were often used in biblical times for the construction of houses, temples, and even palaces. Known for their stability and endurance, these trees can reach up to 120 feet in height and as wide as 30 feet in circumference. Now, for just a moment, close your eyes and imagine yourself standing in a sea of these majestic trees. What a sight to behold the pure beauty of the nature that God created for us to enjoy. Now, imagine a voice so powerful that when spoken, these enormous, strong trees split in half! This is how the psalmist describes the voice of the Lord. A voice that has complete control over the nature that He created. A voice

The Voice

filled with might, yet as peaceful as a dove. A voice that can calm the stormiest of waters. A voice that can bring comfort in mourning. A voice that gives strength to the weak. God says to His people that His sheep recognize His voice. Beloved, God desires us to intimately know His voice. Just as His name is above all names, His voice is above all other voices. Other voices compete for our attention—the enemy, and even ourselves. But there is only One who deserves our undivided attention at all times. His voice alone created the earth and all that it is in it. How powerful is that! He desires such an intimate relationship with us that we recognize and come to appreciate His voice. God says that as we draw near to Him, He will draw near to us. It is in this place that we hear Him, and what a privilege it is to hear from the voice that has nature in His hands.

Spend some time outdoors if you can today, experiencing the beauty of all that He has created. Marvel at His creation and allow yourself to be immersed in His great love for you!

Hidden Treasures

Resurrection Power

> "I want to know Christ—yes, to know the power of his
> resurrection and participation in his sufferings,
> becoming like him in his death, and so, somehow,
> attaining to the resurrection from the dead."
> —Philippians 3:10-11

THE MOMENT YOU accept Christ into your heart, it is a time of renewal. It is the beginning of crucifying an old way of living and living with His resurrection power. There is something so powerful about this beautiful exchange that we often take for granted. In His mercy, God gave His Son's life in exchange for our lives, His perfect life for our marred lives. He, the precious Lamb of God without blemish, we, stained with sin. Yet He invites us to partake of not just His sufferings, but His resurrection. When Jesus rose from the dead, He rose with all power in His hands. There was nothing that the Father withheld from His Beloved Son. If we are partakers with Christ, then we have the same power living within us. This is what makes salvation so amazing—just like Jesus, nothing is withheld from us. We don't have to beg and plead for the power to pray, believe, and receive; it is already there. God says to His people, open your eyes and walk in the authority that was given to you on the day of Christ's resurrection. God says to walk, and better yet, run with it! Attain all that He has for you and believe that what He says about you is true, that His plan for your life will prevail. Remember, He is not asking for you to toil and strive for it, but rather reach for what is already yours.

Pray to the Father that your eyes would be enlightened to the treasure that is within you as a child of the Most High God. Pray that you would have the courage to walk as He says you ought to. Pray that you can trust in His provision; be willing and obedient to heed the call on your life and to do it with power!

Resurrection Power

For His Glory

*"This is to my Father's glory, that you bear much fruit,
showing yourselves to be my disciples."*
—John 15:8

I ABSOLUTELY LOVE the produce section at the grocery store. There's something about seeing fresh fruit and vegetables in a fresh array of colors. The colorful display simply draws me in. Can the same be said of us? Are we such a beautiful display of fruit that others are drawn in? Is God being glorified through our lives? When you are abiding in Christ, the Word says that He then abides in you. In other words, He makes it His business and priority to dwell within you. Just as rain and sunshine cause the fruit of the earth to grow, His presence in our lives causes our spiritual fruit to grow. What does this beautiful display of spiritual fruit look like? Galatians 5:22-23 reminds us that love, joy, peace, patience, kindness, goodness, faithfulness, gentleness, and self-control displayed in us are evidence of His Spirit abiding within us. In addition, a faith that moves mountains, standing on His rich promises, and living in obedience are all considered bearing fruit. Remember, Jesus came to give us life and life abundantly. That abundance comes from living in harmony with Him and obeying Him. You see, by our bearing fruit, others are brought into His kingdom and God is glorified. Beloved, that is why He chose us. We did nothing to be chosen—it was pure love. He chose us to bear fruit for His kingdom and to live lives filled with eternal purpose.

During your prayer time, thank God for choosing you to bear fruit for His kingdom that will bring His name all the glory. Pray for guidance in how He would like to use you for His eternal purposes.

Hidden Treasures

His Holiness

"I call out to the Lord,
and he answers me
from his holy mountain."
—Psalm 3:4

JOHN 1:14 SAYS, "The Word became flesh and made his dwelling among us. We have seen his glory, the glory of the one and only Son, who came from the Father, full of grace and truth." The beauty of salvation is that God in His holiness allowed Himself to become flesh in the person of Jesus Christ to save us from our sins and an eternity separated from Him. He not only chose to lay down His life for us, but He chose to leave us with the Holy Spirit to indwell in us forever! We have been blessed beyond measure with these revelations alone. However, God in His holiness doesn't stop there. When we are stained with sin, crying out to Him to desperately to save us, He hears. He not only hears, but He also moves to action. From a place of virtue, honor, consecration, divinity, and purity to a place of darkness, despair, and death resulting in sin; all to save us! Sometimes I think we forget the holiness of God, how sacred He is. His awesome power causes even the demons to tremble and hide. We, as His children, should stand in awe because when He looks at us, He sees His Son. This is why when we pray we are humbled when He answers.

Take some quiet time and reflect on the holiness of God. Let it lead you to a time of praise and worship before the King. Let it be a time where you worship Him for being all that He is. Thank Him that He answers when you call!

His Holiness

Hannah

"Be joyful in hope, patient in affliction, faithful in prayer."
—Romans 12:12

YEAR AFTER YEAR, she made the trip to Shiloh to make sacrifices unto the Lord. Year after year, she traveled with her adoring husband and his other wife. Year after year, without fail the other wife taunted and ridiculed her because of her barrenness. You see, to be barren in those times was humiliating and disgraceful to a woman. No one saw the heartache that Hannah felt. Even her husband couldn't understand her sadness as he loved her dearly and provided for her every need. But Hannah knew something was missing, that God had not actually called her to be barren. She knew it was just a matter of His timing and trusting that He always heard her prayers. This year, this trip was different, there was a stirring so deep within Hannah that something needed to change, and that change was now. She made her way to the temple, and in bitter anguish in her soul, she cried out to God and said:

> LORD Almighty, if you will only look on your servant's misery and remember me, and not forget your servant but give her a son, then I will give him to the LORD for all the days of his life, and no razor will ever be used on his head."
> —1 Samuel 1:11

She kept on praying until the words became inaudible, weeping uncontrollably with eyes closed, pressing closer and closer to the altar. It was there that Eli the priest took notice of her state and presumed she was drunk. She replied in humility that she was not drunk but only pouring out her heart to the Lord. Eli then blessed her and here is her reply: "She said, 'May your servant find favor in your eyes.' Then she went her way and ate something, and her face was no longer downcast" (1 Samuel 1:18).

Did you catch that? It says that her face was no longer downcast! Earlier that day, she was stricken with shame and a sadness that even her husband couldn't ease, but now she was encouraged and of good cheer. This is the very response our Father is looking for. For us to lay it all out before the throne and walk away encouraged and confident that He hears and will answer.

Beloved, may our prayer posture be like Hannah's, trusting in the One who sees and remembers His child. Hallelujah!

Hidden Treasures

His Faithfulness Endures Forever

"God is not human, that he should lie,
not a human being, that he should change his mind.
Does he speak and then not act?
Does he promise and not fulfill?"
—Numbers 23:19

THROUGHOUT OUR LIVES, so many things change. Sometimes there will be seasons in which we cannot see the way and God simply asks us to trust, leaning not on our own understanding but resting in who He is. He is a constant source of strength, He never changes, and we can trust that. Here are a few reminders of that very truth:

To him who alone does great wonders,
His love endures forever.
who by his understanding made the heavens,
His love endures forever.

who spread out the earth upon the waters,
His love endures forever.
who made the great lights—
His love endures forever.
the sun to govern the day,
His love endures forever.
the moon and stars to govern the night;
His love endures forever.
—Psalm 136:4-9

He remembered us in our low estate
His love endures forever.
and freed us from our enemies.
His love endures forever.
He gives food to every creature.
His love endures forever.
—Psalm 136:23-25

Meditate on what you have just read. Reflect on the faithful love of the Father in your own life. Enter into a time of praise for His unchanging presence in your life…He is worthy!

His Faithfulness Endures Forever

Snooze Button

"Do not love sleep or you will grow poor;
stay awake and you will have food to spare."
—Proverbs 20:13

OKAY, HERE'S A bit of information about me...I enjoy sleep! There's something about being bundled underneath a warm, down comforter with a soft pillow underneath my head. Interestingly enough, the Father knows His daughter; He knows my innermost being, every intricate detail of my existence, including this little fact about me. Yet, He chooses to woo me in the morning, calling me out of my peaceful slumber, asking me not to savor those last few moments of sleep before the morning's activities begin. I confess, sometimes the snooze button gets a little overused. But every morning, He beckons me to spend time in His presence. Not fully awake, I arise and make my way to my "secret place" for fellowship with the Creator of the universe. As I begin to come to my senses, it is then that

I remember He is the bright and morning star. The One who causes the moon to hide and the sun to awaken the dawn. This is where He whispers, "I am the bread of life. Whoever comes to me will never go hungry, and whoever believes in me will never be thirsty" (John 6:35). This is the place where He can fill your cup until it is overflowing. You see, He knows what your day will bring, He knows what you will encounter, and He wants you prepared. He wants you to be able to give a word in due season to someone in need. He wants to encourage, instruct, and sometimes rebuke you in a place where no one else is vying for your attention, just you and the Father. More importantly, it's a time of refreshment in your relationship with Him. He wants to enjoy sweet fellowship with His children. I haven't attained perfection in the morning hours, but I do realize that I must daily crucify my desire for extended sleep and arise when He says arise, He is so worth it!

If you are like me and struggle with morning hours, pray about it. Ask God to show you how to overcome. He may show you, as He did with me, that your nighttime routine needs adjusting. Remember, what He shows you, follow up with obedience.

Hidden Treasures

The Fountain

"May the God of hope fill you with all joy and peace as you
trust in him, so that you may overflow with hope
by the power of the Holy Spirit."
—Romans 15:13

I ONCE VACATIONED at a beautiful resort where everywhere you looked a fountain was in view. Some were big, some were small, but they all carried out the same function. Once the top was filled, the other tiers were filled to overflowing thus emptying into the next and so on. It reminded me of what trusting in God is like. Once you set your hope in the Savior, something begins to happen underneath the surface of your being. There is an inexpressible feeling of joy, of peace, and of hope that begins to unfold before your eyes. Without you even asking for it, it becomes the response of the Holy Spirit working within you. It is a gift from the Almighty, something that you could never obtain through human relationships or circumstances. Beloved, we are His fountains. We were made for His glory. While we are continuously flowing with this hope, He keeps us happy and satisfied. We find ourselves walking in peace through the most difficult of times. Luke 7:38 says, "Whoever believes in me, as Scripture has said, rivers of living water will flow from within them." You see, if we are the fountains, then He is the water flowing through us. This water replenishes, cleanses, and quenches our thirst. It sustains and fills us completely. This is the hope that we cling to!

Spend some time in prayer reflecting on the hope that you have in Christ. Remember, as His fountain, you are to overflow into the lives of those around you. Make a choice to be a blessing to someone this week!

The Fountain

Nothing New

> This is what the LORD says:
> "Stand at the crossroads and look;
> ask for the ancient paths,
> ask where the good way is, and walk in it,
> and you will find rest for your souls.
> But you said, 'We will not walk in it.'"
> —Jeremiah 6:16

THE WORD OF God is unchangeable. It is eternal and holds truths that will last for generations to come. There is a pathway set by God that He has already laid out for His children. A path that leads to righteousness, peace, prosperity, and a rest that only He can give. This is nothing new. When we read about Abraham, Moses, Ruth, Paul, David, and all the others who have gone before us, we see the ancient path that has been laid out for us to walk on. Jesus said, "I am the way and the truth and the life. No one comes to the Father except through me"

(John 14:6). You see, it doesn't just stop there at the point of salvation; it is an ongoing process of living according to God's plan. He came so that we could have life and life in abundance. Make no mistake about it, He has an awesome plan for your life, but you must choose His path and His way. He is faithful to His Word, and He promises to keep you as you follow Him. He will never leave you nor forsake you. When you want peace, follow Him. When you want rest for your weary souls, follow Him. When you want truth, follow Him. There is a path with your name marked on it. He has already paved the way. Study the Word of God and see it, embrace it, and start walking. Believe with all of your heart on the steadfastness of God and His Word. He is the same yesterday, today, and forever.

Beloved, God Himself is the Ancient of Days. He was, He is and He is to come. That is why we can trust in the Word of God for our lives, our children's lives, and our children's children's lives! This is the way we ought to take. When He speaks and shows you the way, take heed!

Hidden Treasures

Family Tree

"Therefore, since we are surrounded by such a great cloud
of witnesses, let us throw off everything that hinders
and the sin that so easily entangles. And let us run
with perseverance the race marked out for us."
—Hebrews 12:1

IN THE BOOK of Hebrews, chapter 11, we are introduced to the "Hall of Faith"—those who by God's grace stood on His promises and moved in obedience to whatever He commanded. They trusted God in spite of imprisonment, beatings, and even death. They held fast to the promises of God. This, beloved, is our heritage. When we put our trust in Christ, we are chosen to be a part of this family. This group of believers has now become our ancestors. They had their eyes fixed on God. They ran their race with endurance. No matter what came, they were faithful to a faithful God. Now, at this very moment, you and I are surrounded by all those who have gone before us showing us the way of faith. This is why reading the Word of God is vital. This is how we grow in our faith, how we see with spiritual eyes how to live for God in a way that defies the natural. It is through the blood of Jesus Christ that we are called to be part of this family. It's in your blood to RUN, not walk with a spirit of perseverance the race before you. Hallelujah! I can just imagine, in heaven, a crowd of our ancestors cheering us on as we race to the finish line, encouraging us every step of the way. Even though you are weary, you can't stop. Beloved, it's in your DNA to win! It's in your blood to endure, to persevere, to keep moving in spite of what may come your way. You have to remove everything that holds you back from pursuing all that the Father has for you. Remove the bad habits, unhealthy relationships and mindsets. Remove anything that is in your way and run your race!

Beloved, God has given us His Word to encourage us. He knows that there will be times when it's hard to take even a baby step. Read his Word and thank God that He has provided everything you need to run the race set before you and know that He has destined for you to win!

Family Tree

Standing in the Gap

> "For if you keep silent at this time, relief and deliverance shall arise for the Jews from another place, but you and your father's family will perish. And who knows but that you have come to the royal position for such a time?"
> —Esther 4:14

THE BOOK OF Esther gives us a glimpse into the sovereignty of God and His power to deliver. We see firsthand a story of God's providential timing and the response of a young Jewish woman who was at the right place at the right time. She went from being a young orphan being raised by her uncle to becoming the Queen of Persia. The path that God had set before her was no coincidence. Boy, did God have an assignment for her! Faced with the possible annihilation of the Jewish people, the burden was laid upon her heart to intervene. Esther wasted no time in asking the king, her husband, to move into action and save her people from this malicious plot. Esther's very life was at stake because her identity as a Jew was not yet made known to the king, yet Esther thought nothing of herself. You see, it was against the law to enter into the king's presence uninvited. So she fasted and prayed and decided that the welfare of her people mattered more than her own life, saying:

> Go, gather together all the Jews who are in Susa, and fast for me. Do not eat or drink for three days, night or day. I and my attendants will fast as you do. When this is done, I will go to the king, even though it is against the law. And if I perish, I perish (Est. 4:16).

In the end, because of Esther's courage, humility, and the awareness of God's timing of her placement within the kingdom, the plot was foiled and the king granted her request to save the Jews. If you have never read the book of Esther, please do so. It is filled with so much more than I have had the chance to share. Beloved, this is what standing in the gap looks like. Take a look around you. Where has God placed you so that you can be His hands and His feet? What is the burden that God has placed upon your heart that requires courage? What is God speaking to your heart that requires an obedience such as Esther's?

Ask that God would enlighten you to the season you are in now and how He wants to use you in the lives of others. When He shows you, trust that He will provide all that you need to carry out this God-sized assignment. He will cover you with a hedge of protection and He will be glorified!

Hidden Treasures

A Steadfast Heart

"And as for you, brothers and sisters,
never tire of doing what is good."
—2 Thessalonians 3:13

I CAN REMEMBER countless days and nights as a young mom often feeling overwhelmed and exhausted. Everything that I was doing was good, all for the welfare of the home and the little people that occupied it. Now, in a different season of life, I can see with spiritual eyes all that God was doing inside of me. He was developing perseverance and the ability to keep moving when I was weak, not losing heart when some deeds went thankless, but to remember that when serving it was unto the Lord. You see, God in His wisdom never misses an opportunity to teach us His lessons. Putting my hope in Him, keeping my eyes fixed on Him, unwavering in my purpose, and cleaving to Him for the strength that only He provides were all things I learned in one season but are now being used in another season.

Whatever He has called you to go through, do not grow weary. Continue moving with a steadfast heart, wholly committed to Him and the purpose that He desires to fulfill in you. Whether it is being a stay-at-home mom or working outside the home, be steadfast. Whether it's in prayer and fasting, be steadfast. Whether it's a time of movement or a time of waiting, be steadfast. Whether it's a time of seeking the Lord for direction or walking in obedience, be steadfast. Know that He does everything with a purpose in mind. Know that He causes all things to come together for your good. Know that when you are weak He is strong and that He never grows weary but He gives limitless strength when you call on His name.

As you pray, thank God that when you are weary, this promise is true for you, "But he said to me, 'My grace is sufficient for you, for my power is made perfect in weakness'" (2 Cor. 12:9).

A Steadfast Heart

Display of Glory

"The heavens declare the glory of God;
the skies proclaim the work of his hands."
—Psalm 19:1

I REMEMBER IT as if it were yesterday. It was a rather stormy day; clouds had taken over, with no sunlight visible to the human eye. It was now evening time and I was headed to a rehearsal. As I was driving I noticed an orange light reflecting off the trees. The light was so bright that I assumed it was a low-flying aircraft, as I live close to a military base, or maybe lighting from a construction zone. As the line of cars in front of me began to move, I was able to see the true source of the light. It was the sun, in the most beautiful hues of orange and red I had ever seen. What a sight! To see the sun's awesome splendor being reflected off of the trees was simply breathtaking. What amazed me more was that after a gloomy, dark day, the sun had finally made its presence known. Beloved, this is the beauty of

God's creation. This is how He communicates through the very nature He created. Just as the sun was out all day long, sitting behind the clouds, God is always there. He is omnipresent. When life gets dark, God is waiting to shine His light upon you. God shows His power when you feel you have done all you can do. You are always surrounded by His glory, but sometimes it takes a season of darkness to see it. This is the beauty of a storm in your life, so that His magnificent glory can be on full display. As you ponder the storms of life, concentrate on all the attributes of God and give Him the glory that is due Him. He is an awesome God!

Spend time in prayer and thank God that throughout every season of life, He is speaking and actively working things out for your good and for His glory. Ask Him to keep your eyes open so that you can readily see Him in the midst of darkness and thank Him for never leaving your side.

Hidden Treasures

The Promise Fulfilled

"Look, I am coming soon! My reward is with me,
and I will give to everyone according to what they have done."
—Revelation 22:12

"THE GRASS WITHERS and the flowers fall, but the word of our God endures forever" (Isa. 40:8). Every word written in the Bible is true and flawless. Every word that He speaks bears fruit. When He speaks, He promises that His words spoken will fulfill His purpose. When the prophets of old told of a Savior who would redeem mankind, it came to pass. When our Savior Jesus walked this earth, He told the disciples what was to come concerning his crucifixion, burial, and resurrection, and it came to pass. Now, as His children, we eagerly await His second coming. There are some in this world who mock His return, while others claim to know what only God can know. His Word gives this reminder, "But about that day or hour no one knows, not even the angels in heaven, nor the Son, but only the Father" (Matt. 24:36). He is a promise keeper, He is faithful and true now and in the ages to come. This is the hope that we have living in a fallen world: that He is coming back for His chosen ones. When He comes, He is looking for the faithful who have held fast to His covenant. He is looking for those who were faithful in prayer. He is looking for those who are waiting with expectation for His return. Are you ready?

In prayer, thank God that by being His child, you have eternal life and that this earthly life is temporary. Thank God for His truth and that it is available to all who seek it. Pray for strength, wisdom, and power to fulfill the mission that He desires for you to fulfill while here on this side of eternity.

The Promise Fulfilled

Hidden Treasures

Precious Sister,

I don't want to take for granted that as you have poured over the pages of this prayer journal, that you have the treasure within you. This treasure is the precious gift of salvation. Jesus said, "I am the way and the truth and the life. No one comes to the Father except through me" (John 14:6).

The gift of salvation is not obtained by being perfect, because there is nothing you and I can do to earn God's perfect love. "For it is by grace you have been saved, through faith—and this is not from ourselves, it is the gift of God—not by works, so that no one can boast" (Eph. 2:8-9).

Because we are sinners, we deserve to be eternally separated from God, but because of His Son's death on the cross, we can have life. "For the wages of sin is death, but the gift of God is eternal life in Christ Jesus our Lord" (Rom. 6:23).

"But God demonstrates his own love for us in this: While we were still sinners, Christ died for us."

—Romans 5:8

Here's the best news you will ever hear...God loves you, for Scripture says, "For God so loved the world that he gave his one and only Son, that whoever believes in him shall not perish but have eternal life" (John 3:16).

Right where you are, you can receive Christ as your Savior by praying this simple prayer:

God, I know that I am a sinner and my sins have separated me from You. I am truly sorry, and now I want to turn away from my life of sin and run to You with a repentant heart. Please forgive me. I believe that Your Son, Jesus Christ, died for my sins, was resurrected from the dead, is alive, and hears my prayer right at this very moment. I invite Jesus to become my Savior and the Lord of my life, to rule and reign in my heart from this day forward. Please send Your Holy Spirit to help me obey You, and to do Your perfect will for the rest of my life. In Jesus's name I pray,

Amen

His Promise to You:
> "If you declare with your mouth, 'Jesus is Lord,' and believe in your heart that God raised him from the dead, you will be saved. For it is with your heart that you believe and are justified, and it is with your mouth that you profess your faith and are saved."
> —Romans 10:9-10

Congratulations…you now have the best treasure that you could ever receive! You are now a part of God's family; this new life is not meant to walk alone. You belong somewhere. There is a body of Christ that God wants you to be a part of. I encourage you to visit some local churches. Find a church home in which you are taught biblical truths and grow into the woman that He created you to be!

Your Sister in Christ,
Sharon Pankey

About the Author

Sharon Pankey is a woman who has decided to say YES to God! God has filled her with a passion to share His amazing love with other women. Through writing and teaching the Word of God, Sharon desires for other women to see what precious jewels they are in God's eyes and to pursue the destiny that He created for them.

To share prayer requests, testimonies, or simply how God has used this book in your life, please e-mail Sharon at:

Sharon Pankey
sharonpankey@msn.com

www.ingramcontent.com/pod-product-compliance
Lightning Source LLC
Chambersburg PA
CBHW020414080526
44584CB00014B/1323